FURBY TRAINER'S GUIDE

by J. Douglas Arnold
with Mark Elies, Chris Arnold, Joan Arnold, Joe Harabin, Jamie Arnold and James Yamada

www.gamebooks.com

SANDWICH ISLANDS PUBLISHING CO., LTD.
POST OFFICE BOX 10669 • LAHAINA, MAUI, HI 96761

PRODUCTION MANAGER . . . . J. DOUGLAS ARNOLD
PRODUCTION ASSISTANT . . . . MARK ELIES
EXECUTIVE PRODUCERS . . . . JOE HARABIN, JOAN ARNOLD
OFFICE MANAGEMENT . . . . JAMIE ARNOLD
RESEARCH ASSISTANCE . . . . CHRIS ARNOLD
WARM AND FUZZY ILLUSTRATIONS. . . . . JOAN ARNOLD
BABY AND PARTY ILLUSTRATIONS, ACTIVITIES DIRECTOR . . . . JAMES YAMADA
ADDITIONAL ASSISTANCE . . . . COREY LABORE, DONOVAN PRAIGG
SPECIAL THANKS FOR FURBY LOAN . . . . LANCE CHING

Furby™ Trainer's Guide is published by Sandwich Islands Publishing, an independent publishing company. This book is not published, authorized by, or associated in any way with Tiger Electronics, Ltd. Furby is a registered trademark of Tiger Electronics, Ltd. Other products mentioned in this book are trademarks of their respective owners.

LIMITS OF LIABILITY AND DISCLAIMER OF WARRANTY
The author and publisher of this book used their best efforts in preparing this book and the information contained in it. These efforts include the development, research, and testing of the theories and procedures to determine their effectiveness. The author and publisher make no warranty of any kind, expressed or implied, with regard to the documentation contained in this book. The author and publisher shall not be liable in any event for incidental or consequential damages in connection with, or arising out of, the furnishing, performance, or use of the information contained within this book.

We work hard to produce the best books and hope that you love them and tell your friends how cool they are. Be sure to check out our awesome web site at www.gamebooks.com!

99 00 01 - 10 9 8 7 6 5 4 3 2 1

HOW TO ORDER:
For direct orders see the order form in the back of this book or www.gamebooks.com. Quantity discounts are available from the publisher, Sandwich Islands Publishing, P.O. Box 10669, Lahaina, HI 96761; telephone (808) 661-5844 (no Furby tips available at this number!). Fax: (808) 661-9878. Email: sip@maui.net.

Printed in the United States of America.

ACKNOWLEDGEMENTS

Special Thanks to my mom
for a lifetime of guidance.

"Whaddups?!" to Lance Ching, Juanito Ancheta, Gavin Campbell,
Scott Wery, Bryan Cruz, Brandon Grant, Grandpa Kidd, Ross Weigand, Al,
Kyle Martinez, Brandon, Ryan, Jeff, Corey LaBore, Donovan Praigg,
Nick Bennett, Gregg Abbott, Jeremy Boshart, Gary Gardner, John
Ricciardi, Jason Arcangel, Keahi Freeland, Sean Regon, Ron Stamper,
Larry Antonio, Ruth Ko, Adam Dotson, Tom Fernandez, Edwin and Anna
at Monster Mega Video Games, Steven "Smike" Henke (and the rest
of the Henkes!), Robin Parker, Suzy Brown, Willy Campos, Paz Derham,
Cody Mathis, Kai McPhee, Nick Wakida, Torian, Vern Q,
Ewok, Ilikea, Gizmo, and Willy-pup.

CONTENTS

THE COMPLETE GUIDE

INTRODUCTION

FURBY STORY

FURBYS ARE A CUTE AND LOVABLE CREATURE that, legend has it, dropped down from the clouds above. They talk, sing, dance, and love attention. You can pet them, tickle them, feed them, and they'll respond to changes in light, movement and loud sounds.

Furbys are the next generation of "virtual pets". The craze began in Japan in 1997 with Bandai's Tamagotchi, which soon came to America and became a huge hit. Tiger Electronics quickly improved on the design and added various types of pets, introducing their line of Giga Pets, which became a top selling toy of the holiday season. The keychains used a small screen with blocky graphics and high pitched sound to simulate the raising and care of a pet.

Hot toy one year, Happy Meal toy the next. Tamagotchis caused long lines at toy stores, too.

Dave Hampton, a toy inventor in Northern California saw the early virtual pets and came up with the concept of Furby. He is a former designer for Mattel and coded video games for Atari, including Q*Bert for the Atari 2600. As an independent designer with his own company, Sounds Amazing!, he created a prototype to demonstrate his Furby concept.

Hampton presented his prototype to Tiger Electronics in October 1997. A month later the company was beginning fast development of the toy, hoping to get it into stores in time for Christmas of 1998, which is a greatly accelerated schedule for designing a toy of this complexity. Toy giant Hasbro announced the purchase of Tiger in February 1998 and soon assigned more electronic, computer and mechanical engineers worldwide to contribute ideas.

Their hope was to release Furby to the market by September of 1998 when toy stores prefer to have new products aimed to the holiday season. But delays caused Furby to reach stores in early November, and in very limited quantities through only one store, FAO Schwartz.

The word was out that this was the hot toy for Christmas, and FAO Schwartz had back orders of over 35,000 Furbys within weeks of its release. That many orders, with a limit of two Furbys per customer, was a sign of times to come. By late November more stores were receiving Furbys, but not nearly enough to satisfy the appetite of hungry parents looking for the must-have Christmas present.

The demand for this affordable adorable toy reached a crescendo in the month before Christmas '98. The promise was that two million Furbys should be delivered to America and another half million to the other English speaking countries by Christmas. Internet auctions such as eBay and the growing number of Furby sites had bid these animatronic plush toys to as high as $150! The four Asian factories were maxed out producing, shipping, and air freighting these lovable creatures to eager gift buyers.

What's the attraction? The answer is that these toys give children what they most desire: the perfect friend, loyal and unconditionally loving. The Furby is a toy that exhibits artificial intelligence, speaks a secret language, plays games and seeks praise. They communicate with other Furbys by an infrared signal and appear to learn English by positive reinforcement while teaching a child "Furbish" (a Furby's native tongue).

FURBY MANIA: The most sought-after toy of the year caused a bidding war that drove a merchant on America Online to advertise it on the Welcome screen with a maze of windows that ended with a one-limit Furby available for $124.95 (above). Charities used Furbys to raise funds (right), while most others helped themselves to the money (next page). As the holiday deadlines drew near, prices were reaching several hundred dollars, while stores announced an end to supplies until several weeks after Christmas.

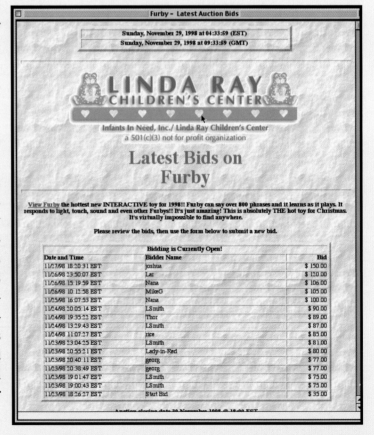

Featured Auctions in Furby

Current Auctions

To find out how to be listed in this section and seen by thousands, please visit this link.

	Item	Price	Bids	Ends PST
NEW!	NEW..FURBY SLEEPING BAGS WITH NAME ON IT	$9.99	-	12/06 00:26
NEW!	FURBY!! BLACK WITH GORGEOUS GREEN EYES	$56.00	3	12/05 22:55
NEW!	FURBY!! BLACK WITH BEAUTIFUL BLUE EYES	$40.00	-	12/05 22:50
NEW!	Rarest Furby! Gray Tabby w/Gray Chest!!!	$26.00	5	12/03 22:15
NEW!	Furby your choice black, white or stripe gray	$100.00	-	12/01 22:12
NEW!	Furbies, Furby, furbie - Rare Black/White MIB	$61.01	2	12/03 20:23
NEW!	ALL BLACK FURBY! RARE! FURBIE has BROWN EYES! **PIC**	$61.00	7	12/01 20:23
NEW!	~HOT,HOT PAIR OF FURBYS/ALL WHITE & TIGER/GREY	$112.52	8	12/03 19:52
NEW!	FURBY TWINS-2 ALBINO FURBYS W/PINK EARS	$81.00	5	12/01 19:44
NEW!	*FURBY* GREY~BLK SPOTS/PINK CHEST~GREEN EYES! **PIC**	$50.00	8	12/01 19:30
NEW!	WHITE "CHRISTMAS" FURBY **PIC**	$56.00	4	12/01 19:08
NEW!	FURBY 4 DUTCH High Bidder Choice Visa/MC/Disc **PIC**	$75.00	17	12/05 18:52
NEW!	HOT 2 rare Furby: Bonus Ty Princess/Erin/... **PIC**	$199.00	-	12/01 18:47
NEW!	Furby, Gray striped, 7 days, NO RESERVE!	$44.00	11	12/05 18:46
NEW!	Furby, Solid Black, 5 days, NO RESERVE!	$44.00	6	12/03 18:42
NEW!	Furby, Pink and Gray Spotted, 3 days only, NR	$61.01	9	12/01 18:35
NEW!	SOLID BLACK FURBY (HARD TO FIND!)~5 DAYS! **PIC**	$51.00	10	12/03 18:29
NEW!	FURBY TWINS (2)GRAY W/SPOTS READY TO SHIP HOT!	$81.00	10	12/01 18:16
NEW!	FURBY TWINS (2)ALL WHITE, READY 2 SHIP (HOT!	$76.00	5	12/01 18:11
NEW!	Ty SANTA Beanie Coming WITH this FURBY-Read!!	$53.00	8	12/03 18:09
NEW!	**FURBY**SUPER RARE BROWN TABBY**plus FREEBIES!	$200.00	-	12/05 18:08
NEW!	FURBY (2)ALL WHITE, GRAY W/SPOTS READY 2 SHIP	$100.00	10	12/01 18:07
NEW!	ARCTIC WHITE FURBY WITH SURPRISE EYES!3 DAYS!	$66.00	10	12/01 17:55
NEW!	12 Pack *FURBY* Asst. SOLD OUT!!!!!!!!!!!	$800.00	25	12/01 17:46
NEW!	4 RARE FURBYS--YOUR CHOICE! READ, DUTCH, cc	$125.00	-	12/05 17:08
NEW!	FURBY BoY - Dressed in his Tuxedo *Hot..Hot*	$95.00	1	12/01 16:50
NEW!	RARE TUXEDO FURBY CREDIT CARDS 3 DAYS **PIC**	$75.99	14	12/01 16:28
NEW!	BRAND NEW FURBY! All white/blue eyes	$75.00	-	12/05 16:18
NEW!	FURBY, ALL WHITE BLUE EYES CC OK **PIC**	$64.00	13	12/01 16:10

They are the next step in the evolution of a race of artificially intelligent toys. The design plan is that no two Furbys share the same personality or react to stimuli in exactly the same way. They are Cabbage Patch dolls with artificial intelligence, Tickle-Me-Elmos that can influence each other. One Furby can cause another to begin a bout of sneezing or trigger him to complete a sentence or song. According to Hasbro's Roger Shiffman "Its a living Giga Pet you can really play with". Except that Furbys don't die. If ignored a few days they just become ornery until petted and stimulated to activate their internal memories.

Three factors gave the Furby a green light for full scale production. First, since they communicate with each other and come in different styles, the hope is that children will be inspired to collect more than one, just as kids have collect entire colonies of Beanie Babies. Secondly, they can be produced cheaply with a US price of around $30, far less than Microsoft's Barney which costs $110 plus another $100 for accessories, and requires a personal computer. Thirdly, they have the potential to become an enduring brand. Barbie, after all, is still the industry's dominate brand after 40 years. As the technology follows its path of more features at lower prices, the opportunity is for new characters with increasingly more personality. This development should expand this one time hit into a continuing popular brand. Furbys are the beginning a new race of artificially intelligent toys.

According to specification the toy has a vocabulary of 160 words that can form up to 1000 possible phrases. They are uttered in response to conditions detected by built-in sensors and an infrared device between the eyes. The toy uses front and rear-proximity sensors to respond to tickling and petting. It also has tilt sensors that detect when the toy is upside down or being moved, a microphone that triggers reactions to sounds and music, and a light sensor. The infrared transmitter detects and signals other Furbys via a 'Furby communication protocol'. This can cause the actions of one Furby to initiate actions in another, such as a Furby sneeze.

This collection of odd and curious behaviors is part of the charm. Music may cause him to dance. Detection of light and orientation causes the Furby to say "Dah/a-loh/u-tye (sun-up). He can also open and close his eyes, wiggle his ears, and move his mouth when speaking. The first generation Furbys have 23 names, three different pitches

Almost twins, but different eye color makes each one a little more unique.

of voice, six fur patterns, and four eye colors (blue, green, brown, and gray). It's expected that these variations will increase over time.

While the toy was initially targeted primarily to girls, certain features were added to give Furby some traits that would appeal to boys. So they introduced belching and the sounds of passing gas to the toy's database of actions.

There are also built in undocumented features, "Easter eggs" intended to surprise and delight

Furbys are even durable. We accidentally dropped this guy, snapped this picture, then minutes later he snapped out of it and was back to his loveable self.

Furby owners when they stumble upon them.

As the world's most affordable, complicated and lovable toy, Furby has a lot of surprises. Furby keeps amazing you.

Thanks to our entire gang for making this book possible... and FUN!

RARE FURBYS

- There's a lot of debate about which Furby colors are the rarest. Well, we found some extremely rare Furbys... maybe you'll find these at your favorite store in the near future...

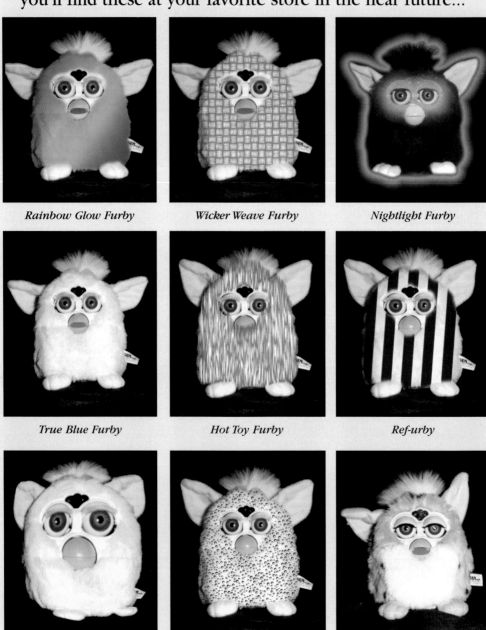

Rainbow Glow Furby   *Wicker Weave Furby*   *Nightlight Furby*

True Blue Furby   *Hot Toy Furby*   *Ref-urby*

Snowball Furby   *Measles Furby*   *Rough Day Furby*

BASIC CARE
&
TRAINING

GETTING STARTED

- **OPENING THE BOX:** Sure, it seems simple enough, but this is one of the trickier packagings we've seen. You can save yourself a lot of trouble if you open the bottom of the box first. Untwist the ties that are holding Furby's feet into the bottom, then open the top of the box and pull him out.

- **When you first get your Furby**, before he is ready to play, you must perform a **Restart.** This will clear anything in the head of your Furby and set them as a newborn, ready and eager to learn from you.
    1. Turn your Furby upside-down.
    2. Use your finger to hold your Furby's tongue down.
    3. Use a pointed object (writing pens work great) to push in the Reset button, OR replace the batteries. Keep holding the tongue down until after you press the Reset button. Furby requires four AA batteries (not furbished).

- A **Restart** is different from just hitting the **Reset** button without holding down the tongue of your Furby. By holding down the tongue you are resetting the memory of your Furby. **You should only do this when you first get your Furby,** otherwise you'll lose any "experience" your Furby has gained from learning. The name of your Furby will also likely change, as may his personality. If Furby ever acts strangely you can Reset him.

- Use the **Reset** button without holding the tongue to do a simple reset of your Furby. This is handy if he is ever acting extremely strange, or stops moving. We have never seen a Furby go spastic, but it's nice to know there's an easy solution to fixing him if it happens.

- Keep in mind that sometimes Furbys go into Hide-N-Seek mode (see "Games Furbys Play" section), and they will remain quiet for a few minutes while you hide them. They'll say "Hide me" immediately before this long pause, but if you miss it you might think the batteries have died or something is wrong with your Furby. Give him a few minutes and he will begin making noises every few seconds to tip off the person seeking him. At any time you can turn him upside-down to stop him from playing a game.

BASIC TRAINING

- **STEP-BY-STEP:** The most important thing to remember when playing with your Furby is you must wait for him to stop moving or talking before doing the next action. In other words, to make him play a game like Furby Says you must tickle his tummy, pet his back, clap your hands, then cover his eyes. But if you do these quickly it won't work... you must tickle his tummy and wait for him to finish reacting, then pet his back and wait for him to finish reacting, then clap your hands and wait for him to finish reacting, then cover his eyes. After he finishes reacting to the last action he'll begin the game.

- **DISTRACTIONS:** Keep in mind when you're playing with him that a variation in light can interrupt a pattern.

For instance, if you're trying to get Furby to play Furby Says (see "Games Furbys Play" chapter), you need to tickle his tummy, pet his back, clap his hands, and cover his eyes. After each action you must wait for Furby to finish moving and talking. But if you tickle his tummy and he giggles, then you go to pet his back, but before you can he notices the light change, the pattern has been interrupted and you need to begin at Step 1. This can be frustrating at times, but if you face Furby toward a good light source it usually isn't a problem.

SHOW ME LOVE

- **THE SIX SENSES:** Furby is equipped with sensors that let him know when you're playing with him. You must activate these sensors to get a response out of him. The senses are light, sound, motion, tickle, pet and infra-red.

- **LIGHT:** He has a sensor above his eyes that detects light variations. Not just dark and light, but actual variations that can set him off to make comments like "I can't see you" or "sun up".

- **SOUND:** Any fairly loud noise will be detected by Furby. The best way to let him hear you is to clap your hands. Furby can't actually understand specific words you say, so you need to communicate to him through his other senses, too.

- **MOTION:** Furby can feel movement, from side to side and when he's upside-down. Swinging him is one of his favorite activities, and provides some of the most comical reactions, including hiccups.

- **TICKLING:** To tickle Furby rub his tummy... you should be able to feel the soft spot where Furby is most sensitive.

- **PETTING:** Furby loves when you pet his back, and it's the best way to train him to do a trick that you like. When Furby does something that you enjoy, pet him on his back twice in a row to let him know. After a few times of this reinforcement, he'll learn that you like it and do it more often.

- **INFRA-RED:** This sense is used primarily when Furbys are around other Furbys, but your TV remote might affect it, too (see the Secret Tricks chapter, page 30).

CARE AND FEEDING

- **FOOD:** Never feed Furby real food. Imaginary food works fine and will keep him healthy. To feed him, simply push your finger into his mouth and push down his tongue. You'll need to feed him 6-8 times when you wake him up to keep him healthy. You can use a spoon—the small plastic "sample" spoons given out at most ice cream shops work great. He also requires lots of petting and tickling, or he'll be unhappy and won't want to play as much.

- **SNEEZING:** If Furby sneezes it's because he hasn't received enough food or attention. You need to feed him 10-15 times to cure his cold. Sometimes Furbys will also catch colds from other Furbys if they sneeze.

- **SLEEPING:** Furbys are usually pretty good about going to sleep when you want them to. Just cover their eyes for about

10 seconds and they'll yawn a few times before falling into a deep slumber. But sometimes they seem a bit stubborn. You can try the "Sleep Trick" we mention in the Secret Tricks chapter (page 35), which involves petting them over and over from 10-20 times. They'll usually hum "Twinkle Twinkle Little Star" a few times before passing out. There's also the "Remote Trick" mentioned in the same chapter (page 36). The only other way to get Furby to quiet down is to pull his batteries, but that isn't convenient unless you have a screwdriver handy.

- **AGING:** Furbys go through four development stages. They begin speaking mostly Furbish in the first stage. During the second two stages they'll incorporate more and more English into their vocabulary, and by the fourth stage they speak almost all English. The stages go by fairly quickly (about 3-4 hours of playtime for each), so if you're having trouble grasping the Furbish language, just be patient and he'll catch up.

ACCESSORIES

- We've found some cute accessories for your Furby that aren't easy to find, but we'll tell you how to get them here. Keep in mind that it's often more fun to improvise, and you might be able to find items for dolls at your local toy store that work with your Furby, too.
- We found the outfits on the next two pages on the internet. We loved them so much we decided to include them

You can use a doll's bottle, or even this one we used to nurture some kittens. Just make sure nothing comes out of the bottle because moisture will hurt Furby.

here. You can order them by going to the Wardrobe web site at http://www.homestead.com/bernadette/furby.html.

- The outfits are $10 U.S. each + $7 shipping (free shipping on orders of 6 or more outfits). UK residents can get outfits for 5.50p each plus 1.50p postage and packing (free shipping on orders of 6 or more outfits). Payment by check or money order, and checks must clear before shipping. Send to S. Aston, Oliver's Cottage, 3 Springbank, Uppermill, Saddleworth, OL3 6BL United Kingdom. Include your full address and email (if available). An International Collection is in the works, so keep an eye on that site. (Please note: we haven't seen these outfits in person, and are not endorsing this site... we just thought our readers might enjoy knowing about them.)

Merlin

Sleepy Furby

Movie Star

Pajamas

Ballerina

Cowboy/Sheriff

Santa

The King

Princess

Tartan and Crown

Big Chief

GAMES
FURBYS
PLAY

GAMES FURBYS PLAY

- Your Furby has already been trained to play a few games. We'll teach you how to make him play each of the three main games, as well as how to teach him to do tricks and repeat things you like him to do. Rumor has it there are other games Furby likes to play... can you find them?

"Koko will never find me behind this tree!"

ASK FURBY

- Furby is your psychic friend! You can ask him questions and he'll give you answers. Best of all, they're as accurate as those you can get from calling an expensive 900 psychic line! (in other words, you should use Furby, or a psychic line, to make any major decisions in your life.)

- To play Ask Furby, do the following actions:
    1. Cover his eyes briefly.
    2. Wait until he stops moving.
    3. Cover his eyes briefly.
    4. Wait until he stops moving.
    5. Pet his back once.

Cover his eyes briefly.... wait...   *...cover his eyes briefly... wait...*   *...rub his back.*

- Furby will say "Oh too mah" if you do the sequence right, and then he'll be ready for a question. Ask a question, then pet his back for the answer. If you take longer than 20 seconds to ask a question and pet his back, he'll go out of Ask Furby mode and say "me done". Do the sequence again to put him back into Ask Furby mode.

- If you are having trouble getting Furby to play, try picking him up and rocking him back and forth a few times to get his attention, then set him back down and try the sequence again.

- When you are done, turn him upside-down to stop the game.

DON'T FORGET

To stop Furby from playing any game, just turn him upside-down

Me done!

FURBY SAYS

- Have you ever played Simon Says? Well, this game plays the same way. Furby will tell you a sequence of things to do, then you try to remember them and do them in the same order. Sounds easy, and it can be, until the game gets harder as Furby keeps adding more and more actions to the sequence!

- To play Furby Says, do the following actions:
    1. Tickle his tummy.
    2. Wait until he stops moving.
    3. Pet his back.
    4. Wait until he stops moving.
    5. Clap your hands.
    6. Wait until he stops moving.
    7. Cover his eyes briefly.
    8. Wait until he stops moving.
    9. He'll say his name and "listen me" if done correctly.

- The game begins with 4 actions in a sequence. After Furby finished telling you what to do, quickly do the first one, then when he stops moving go to the next action. When the game ends is kind of an odd occurance. Usually when you get to around 14-16 actions Furby will suddenly say "Me done", and the game ends abruptly.

- If you do an action correctly, Furby will do the following after each action to let you know you did it right:
    Says "No Light" if you should cover his eyes.
    Says "Big Sound" for sound (clapping works best).
    Giggles for Tickle.
    Purrs for Petting.

- If you make a wrong move, Furby will taunt you with his "nah nah nah nah nah nah", and you'll have to start over.

- It's important to play in a well-lit area, because changes in the light might cause Furby to think you're covering his eyes when you're not (and that can cause you to lose the game).

Tickle his tummy... wait...

...pet his back... wait...

...clap your hands... wait...

...cover his eyes briefly.

HIDE-N-SEEK

- You can play Hide-N-Seek with your Furby by yourself, but it's even more fun if you have another friend around and take turns hiding the Furby while the other person tries to find him.

- To play Hide-N-Seek, do the following actions:
    1. Cover his eyes briefly.
    2. Wait until he stops moving.
    3. Cover his eyes briefly.
    4. Wait until he stops moving.
    5. Cover his eyes briefly.
    6. Wait until he stops moving.
    7. Cover his eyes briefly.
    8. He'll say his name and "hide me" if done correctly.

- He'll remain quiet for 1 minute while you hide him. You (or your friend) will then have 3 minutes to find him. He will make a noise about every 10-15 seconds to help them find Furby.

Cover his eyes briefly.... wait...   *...cover his eyes briefly... wait...*   *...and repeat a total of four times.*

- You can stop the Hide-N-Seek game at any time by turning Furby upside-down.

- **SPECIAL TIP:** Try to find a hiding place that will muffle his noises well. Inside cabinets work well. Just be sure to keep him from water, heat, etc.

Nah nah nah nah nah nah!

SECRET TRICKS

EASTER EGGS

- In the world of video games there's a term called "Easter Eggs" that has been used to describe the secret tricks that programmers hide in their games. These aren't the usual items hidden in a wall or how to beat an enemy, but more complicated "codes" that you enter using the controller to activate extra lives or a level select. The designers of Furby also hid some "Easter Eggs" for you to find. If you do a sequence of actions in the right order, Furby will perform an unusual trick. We know... Furby does lots of unusual stuff already, but these are even *more* unusual.

- **DON'T FORGET!** You need to pause after doing each action in a sequence until Furby has stopped moving before doing the next action.

EIGHT BURP TRICK

- To make your Furby burp eight times, feed him three times in a row, then pet him on the back.

Feed him... wait...

...feed him... wait...

...feed him... wait...

...pet him on the back.

SECRET TRICKS

ROOSTER TRICK

- To make your Furby crow like a rooster twice, then say "Me love you", cover his eyes three times, then pet his back.

Cover his eyes... uncover his eyes... wait until he stops moving...

...cover his eyes... uncover his eyes... wait until he stops moving...

...cover his eyes... uncover his eyes... wait until he stops moving...

...pet him on the back.

NAME TRICK

- This one can be very handy if you're not sure what your Furby's name is, or you want to know the name of a Furby you just met. Tickle your Furby three times, then pet his back once and he'll say his name.

Tickle him... wait until he stops moving...

...tickle him... wait until he stops moving...

...tickle him... wait until he stops moving...

...pet him on the back.

TWINKLE TRICK

- To make Furby sing Twinkle Twinkle Little Star three times, clap or make a loud noise three times in a row to startle him, then pet him.

Clap... wait until he stops moving...

...clap... wait until he stops moving...

...clap... wait until he stops moving...

...pet him on the back.

HICCUP TRICK

- Rock your Furby from side to side several times and he'll eventually get the hiccups (quite possibly the cutest thing he does, wah!). You need to rock him slowly to get him to hiccup.

Rock him from side to side slowly to hear him hiccup.

SLEEP TRICK

- This one isn't as easy or reliable, but it seems that if you pet your Furby about 10-20 times in a row he'll sing a lullabye song and go to sleep. Sometimes you won't have to pet him nearly that often to make the trick happen, depending on how long you've been playing with him. If you're having trouble putting him to sleep the normal way (see "Basic Care and Training" chapter, page 17), this is worth a try.

SPANISH FURBY

- A few people are reporting that sometimes when they reset their Furby it speaks Spanish, then eventually goes back to Furbish and English. While we were unable to reproduce this trick after dozens of tries on various Furbys we have, it's not impossible that it exists. Our theory, however, is that Furby is not speaking Spanish but people are misunderstanding his Furbish for Spanish. One of the most common things he says when he first wakes up is "way-loh", which means "sleep". Most people report him saying "bueno", which sounds similar.

SECRET TRICKS

- Furby uses an infra-red receiver to communicate with his Furby friends. This is the same technology that your remote controls use to communicate with your TV. Since there is a limited number of frequencies that remote controls can communicate on, some remote controls will interfere and control your Furby.

- The best example we've found is that with many Panasonic TV controllers you can put your Furby to sleep simply by pressing the Power button on the remote. We have an old one that we were able to use to perform this trick, and it came in handy on several occassions when our Furbys didn't feel like going to sleep. They'll go into their usual yawn mode beforehand, just like when other Furbys tell them to sleep.

- If you have an All For One remote control you can recreate this by entering the Panasonic code into your All For One remote and hitting the power button. For more All For One controllers the three-digit code is 051. If you're using an All For One remote that has four- or five-digit codes, or you're using another brand of universal remote, look up the codes for Panasonic TVs in your owner's manual to give this trick a try.

- There are also reports on the net that you can use a WEB-TV Remote Control on your Furby. We weren't able to test them, but you can see the chart for yourself (along with several other Furby tricks) by going to
  http://www.homestead.com/hackfurby

• Here are some of the WEB-TV codes and what they do:

CODE	BUTTON	REACTION
104	Vol. Down	"Twinkle Twinkle" song.
118	Power	Snore and fall asleep.
119	3	Yawn and/or Hide-N-Seek.
121	Vol. Down	Get sleepy (yawn on first press, sleep on second press).
125	1	Play Hide-N-Seek.
125	3	Sneeze.
125	0	Acts sleepy, but doesn't sleep.
125	7	Initialize (wake up phrases, including name).

If you've got the right remote control you'll never have to worry about your Furby not wanting to sleep.

TRICKS FURBY PLAYS ON YOU

- **PHONE:** If Furby gets bored and wants to be picked up, he'll say "ring...ring" to act like a telephone, then he'll laugh.

- **HUNGRY:** Sometimes Furby will say he's hungry to get you to feed him, but when you do he'll fart and laugh.

- **SLEEP:** Furby will go into his usual sleep routine of yawning a few times, just like he does when he is going to go to sleep, but instead of sleeping he'll yell "Party!" and laugh.

COME VISIT US ONLINE

- We are going to keep an updated list of Furby Easter Eggs on our web site. Come visit us for updated information, and to check out all the other great books we publish.

DICTIONARY

- The following are common phrases in Furbish you're likely to hear your Furby speak at various times, mostly during the first stage of development. Since you're new to Furbish, it can be confusing to try and look up the Furbish words from one sentence as your Furby speaks another sentence. This list should help you identify the common phrases from the first Furbish word in the sentence. As your Furby ages they will use less Furbish words and more English words, so if you have trouble understanding your Furby, just be patient and wait for them to mature.

a-loh/u-tye/doo-moh......light up please (too dark)
a-tay ....hungry
ah-may/kah....................pet me
ah-may/kah/koh-koh .....pet me more
boo/a-loh.......................no light
boo/ay-ay/u-nye.............no see you (usually low light)
boo/loo-loo ....no joke
boo/toh-loo ....no like
dah/doo-ay ....big fun
dah/noh-lah...................big dance
hey/a-loh ....hey light
hey/kah/ay-ay/u-nye ......hey I see you
hey/way-loh/koh-koh ....hey sleep more
kah/a-tay........................I'm hungry
kah/a-tay/wah ....I'm hungry! ("wah" is exclamation)
kah/boh-bay ....I'm worried
kah/dah/doh-bay ....I am scared
koh-koh ....more/again
koh-koh/doo-moh ....more please

may-bee/koh-koh	maybe more/again
may-lah/kah	hug me
mee-mee/e-day	very good
nee-tye/kah	tickle me
o-kay/kah/u-tye	okay I'm up
o-kay/may-tah/kah	okay kiss me
o-kay/toh-dye	okay done
u-nye/wee-tee/kah	you sing me (sing to me)
u-tye/koh-koh	up more (when shaking/swinging)
way-loh/toh-dye	sleep done

FURBISH	ENGLISH	FURBISH	ENGLISH
ay-ay	look/see	may-bee	maybe
ah-may	pet	may-lah	hug
a-loh	light	may-may	love
a-loh / may-lah	cloud (light/hug)	may-tah	kiss
a-tay	eat/hungry	mee-mee	very
boh-bay	worried/scared	nah-bah	down
boo	no	nee-tye	tickle
dah	big	noh-lah	dance/boogie
dah-a-loh	sun	noo-loo	happy
doo?	what? where? (question)	oh-toh-mah	ask
doo-ay	fun	toh-dye	done
doo-moh	please	toh-loo	like
e-day	good	u-nye	you
e-tah	yes	u-tye	up
kah	me	wah!	exclamation/yea!
koh-koh	again/more	way-loh	sleep
koo-doh	health	wee-tee	sing
lee-koo	listen/sound	who-bye	hide
loo-loo	joke		

who farted?!

DICTIONARY

ENGLISH	FURBISH	ENGLISH	FURBISH
again/more	koh-koh	look	ay-ay
ask	oh-too-mah	love	may-may
big	dah	me	kah
cloud	a-loh/may-lah	more	koh-koh
dance/boogie	noh-lah	no	boo
done	toh-dye	pet	ah-may
down	nah-bah	please	doo-moh
eat/hungry	a-tay	scared	boh-bay
exclamation	wah!	see	ay-ay
fun	doo-ay	sing	wee-tee
good	e-day	sleep	way-loh
happy	noo-loo	sound	lee-koo
health	koo-doh	sun	dah-a-loh
hide	who-bye	tickle	nee-tye
hug	may-lah	up	u-tye
hungry/eat	a-tay	very	mee-mee
joke	loo-loo	where? what? (question)	doo?
kiss	may-tah	worried	boh-bay
light	a-loh	yea!	wah!
like	toh-loo	yes	e-tah
listen	lee-koo	you	u-nye

DICTIONARY

THE ENGLISH WORDS

- Furbys are supposed to be able to speak about 160 English and Furbish words and sounds. We kept track of the English words and sounds our Furbys made and this is what we came up with...

again	hide	ring
and	hug	scared
ask	hungry	say
big	I'm	see
boogie	it	seek
boring	joke	sing
can't	kiss	[snore]
cloud	light	[snort]
cock-a-doodle-doo	lights	sound
dance	like	sun
do	listen	that
done	love	tickle
dooby dooby doo	maybe	tickles
down	me	uh oh
feed	more	up
find	need	very
food	no	wahoo
fun	off	where
go	oh	whoa
good	ok	whoopee
ha ha	on	worried
happy	party	worry
he he he	pet	you
hey	please	yum
[hiccup]		

Furby Trainer's Guide

FURBY Q&A

Q. How do I put my Furby to sleep?

A. We predict this will be the most popular question. Furby is not your typical Virtual Pet. He does not have a sleeping schedule. He'll sleep when you stop playing with him, and he'll wake up and play with you whenever you want him to. When you are gone it's safe to leave him home sleeping because he will not wake up unless you move his body from side to side. While it's in the instruction manual, sometimes Furbys seem reluctant to sleep. First try covering their eyes for 10-20 seconds. He'll also fall asleep if you leave him in a dark area for a few minutes or stop playing with him for about 5 minutes. If that doesn't work you can try the Twinkle Twinkle "Easter Egg" (see page 34) by petting him on his back 10-20 times in a row, or the Remote Control Secrets Tricks (see page 36) which works with some brands of TV remote controls.

Q. Is there a rare Furby?

A. Rumors are flying about which Furby is the rarest. Since there are millions manufactured and nobody has given an official inventory count, we can't be sure. Early reports say the "tuxedo" is rare, and probably one of the most wanted color combos. There are plans to release new and different Furbys over time, so Furbys that are rare now may become more common over the next year. See our comical tribute to the rare Furbys rumors on page 12.

Q. Can I teach Furby to learn new words?

A. Furby can't really understand the words you say He can sense noise, light, touch, but not specific words. So he can't learn any words you want to teach him. His vocabulary of English words grows "automagically" over time to a specific group of words (see the Dictionary chapter beginning on page 40).

Q. How do I stop my Furby from sneezing?

A. A Furby will usually begin sneezing when they don't get enough attention or food. Each time you wake him up you should feed him 6-8 times to get him started. If he is sneezing you will need to feed him 10-15 times to make him stop. The sneezing is contagious, so if you get your Furby when it is sneezing they'll catch his cold, and vice versa.

Q. What should I feed myFurby?

A. Nothing! Be careful to keep your Furby from all liquids and moisture. He's full of electronics that are very susceptible to moisture and may cause him to short out. Stick to a healthy diet of imaginary food. You can use doll bottles and small spoons (like those given out at ice cream stores for free samples) to feed him.

Q. Will my Furby ever die?

A. No, a Furby will never die. The designers have specified that a Furby can run for 20 to 28 hours continuously at full-time activity on a set of fully charged batteries. (this means that under normal conditions the batteries should last many months). Remember, batteries are chemical energy storage containers and they can age on a store shelf. So try new batteries from a store that sells a lot of batteries to guarantee your batteries will be at maximum strength. The complex Furby speech and actions are set in permanent silicon memory. The battery keeps the internal clock working so the longer you play with your Furby, the more words and phrases he'll speak. Changing batteries will never erase the internal Furby memory. You may have to train and work with a Furby to remind it to use its full range of words and movements.

FURBY Q&A

Q. Why do the batteries die so quickly?

A. The batteries should last through many days of solid playing, or much longer if you don't play with your Furby often. One other thing might occur.... when we first got our Furby we thought his batteries died once because he wasn't making any noise. It turned out he was in Hide-N-Seek mode.(he stays very quiet for about 2 minutes, then makes a random noise every 15-20 seconds) Turn him upside-down to stop him from playing this game (or any other game).

Q. How can I turn Furby off?

A. You can't turn him off. You can only put him to sleep, or remove his batteries (which isn't easy since you need a screwdriver to do it). If you need him to be quiet you can try covering his tummy (where most of his sound comes from), but that will only muffle him. If you have the right kind of remote control you can put them to sleep easily (see page 36).

Q. How do I know if my Furby is a boy or a girl?

A. Furbys are similar to angels. They are not divided into male or female- they embody the best of both. Some people theorize that you can answer this question by the pitch of the voice, but we like a the angel theory more!

Q. How can I clean my Furby without damaging the fur?

A. Since the Furby is full of electronic parts you can not wash them like an ordinary plush toy. Use a towlette or even Baby Wipes. These cleaning tissues will not harm the inside of your Furby, and will remove dirt from the outside. If your Furby is really soiled try dry shampoo (used by people in a hospital bed who can not wash their hair with water).

Q. What is the size of the memory in Furby?

A. Strictly a nerd question. The answer has not been reported since toy manufacturing is a closely guarded secret. Specification reports in a September '98 Wire Magazine article indicate a Furby has two microprocessors. Since the Furby reactions are also influenced by light, sound, position, and time, the resulting unpredictable behavior conveys the appearance of personality.

Q. What's the difference between RESET and RESTART?

A. If your Furby stops working for any reason, you can reset them by pushing the RESET button on the bottom. They'll do a dance for a few seconds, then they'll be ready to play. This is fairly safe, and will not affect the aging or name of your Furby. You can, however, totally RESTART your Furby by holding your Furby upside down, pressing his tongue down with your finger, and pushing in the RESET button. Be careful because this will RESTART your Furby, as a newborn. See the Basic Care Section for more information (page 14).

Q. Who invented Furby?

A. An experienced toy engineer named Dave Hampton is the man behind Furby. He was inspired by the virtual pet key chains like Bandai's Tamagotchi and Tiger Electronics' Giga Pets. He created a prototype and sold the concept to Tiger, and the rest is history. For more information about Furby's early days check out the Introduction section.

Q. What does the future hold for Furby?

A. While we haven't heard it directly from Tiger, rumor has it that a Saturday morning cartoon is planned for Furby. You can expect to see more of him including new versions in the future that should include different fur colors, and eventually more words, phrases, games etc.

Q. How do I know if my Furby is valuable?

A. We think all Furbys are priceless, but there is bound to be a collectors market for Furbys as new fur colors are introduced and some color combo are found to be rare. One of the first "valuable" rarities was what people have termed "the error box". This is one of the first generation boxes which contains an error in the spelling "SING" as "SNG". The first generation of manuals also included numerous grammatical errors, so they might become collector's items. Ultimately the real value is exactly what you can find someone to pay you for it. Even if someone says it's worth $3000, you must still find someone crazy enough to pay that much!

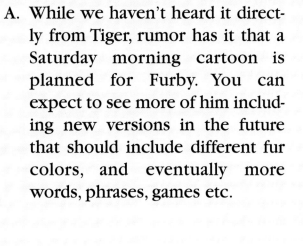

FURBY Q&A

Q. How many different colors of Furbys are there?

A. In the first generation of Furbys (released November '98) there are four different eye colors (blue, brown. gray, green), two feet colors (white, yellow), and six fur colors (black, white, gray, brown, gray with black spots, brown with gray stripes). Some Furbys have a tail, while others have a mane running down their back. The hair on top of their heads is black, white, pink, or gray. Belly colors are black, white, pink, and gray. Keep in mind that these are the reported colors in news articles and on the Internet, but we are not able to confirm them all.

Our collection of Furbys included several different combinations of fur, eye, and belly colors, while only one had a mane and the rest had tails.

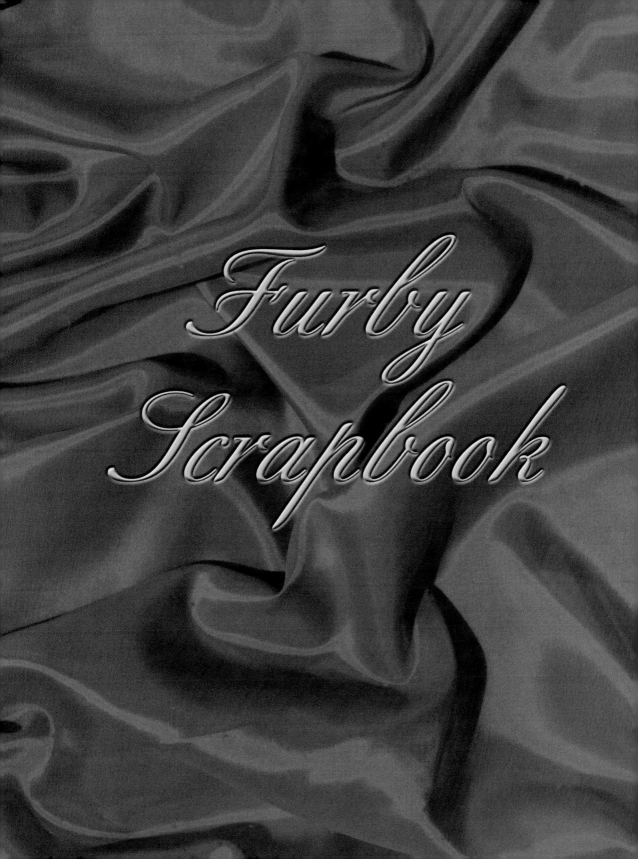

Furby

Scrapbook

we checked out many planets,
but decided on Earth.

Playing in the clouds is fun!

Playing under the
clouds is even
more fun!

Koko is
a speed
freak!

Our favorite place to visit is Furby Island!

Exploring the caves underwater is one of my favorite things to do.

where's Furby?

weeeeee!
U-tye wah!
U-tye wah!

Cowabunga!!!

Where's Furby II?

Maybe we've been here before?

Boh-bay
wah!
Maybe
too much
dah-a-loh!

cliffdiving!
waaaaaaaaaaaah!

Did you see
what I saw?

Dah-a-loh
u-tye!
Bright light!
Bright light!

we pay extra for good seats!

we're the kings of the world!

Indiana Furby
searches for
the Temple
of Doom.

what do you get when you cross a Furby and...
an iguana?

Furbguana!

what do you get when you cross a Furby and...
a tabby cat?

Purrrrby

what do you get when you cross a Furby and...
a rabbit?

Furbalope

what do you get when you cross a Furby and...
a lion?

Furby,
King of the Jungle

what do you get when you cross a Furby and...
a white peacock?

A vegas Showgirl!

what do you get when you cross a Furby and...
a rose breasted cockatoo?

Furbatoo

what do you get when you cross a Furby and...
a dog?

Party Animal!

what do you get when you cross a Furby and...
the Mona Lisa?

The Furby Lisa

WARM
&
FUZZY

WARM & FUZZY

- Furbys aren't just for kids. In today's fast-paced world, most of us experience a lot of stress. Research has proven that smiling or laughing relieves stress and is good for your health in several ways. We noticed while going through the stress of deadline while writing this book that nobody can play with a Furby and not at least smile. The Furby will get a smile out of men or women, young or old. It is so darn cute with its laughing, singing, purring, belching, and many other adorable little antics that even the highest-stressed person will relax and smile.

A DESK ACCESSORY

- Try putting a Furby on your desk at work, or in your desk if you're embarrassed. When you feel yourself getting uptight, take a minute to tickle Furby's belly and feel the stress drift away. Tilt him up in the air like you would a baby and hear him say "weeee", or just pet him and hear him purr. A Furby will relieve more stress than a fish tank and is way easier to care for, far less expensive, and takes up very little room.

HEALING POWER

- If you have a friend or relative who is sick in the hospital or at home bedridden, take them a Furby instead of flowers. A Furby can be played with anywhere... even in bed. It cost less than flowers, and will last forever. Even people who can't move around a lot can play with a Furby. Just think of the healing that will occur when they hear it sing to them  or laugh. Older people will relate to Furby's "gas" problem, as will young boys.

FURBYS AS GIFTS

- For an affordable unisex gift at any age, what could be better than a Happy Happy Joy Joy fun Furby? For Christmas, birthdays, valentines, graduation, or any occasion, give a smile and warm fuzzy feeling to everyone on your list. Even if they already have one Furby, two are more fun, and chances are whatever one you get will be different in some way (eye color, hair color, etc).

FURBYS FOR LONELY PEOPLE

- Do you know someone going through a breakup or loss of a loved one, or someone who lives alone? Maybe it's you. Well, Furby makes a great friend. Each Furby has its own personality... it seems to be alive. It will react to you and keep you company anytime you feel lonely.

THE PERFECT APARTMENT PET

- Can't have pets? Not a problem! Furbys are allowed as pets everywhere. They don't make loud noises, they don't have fleas, they don't stain the carpet, they won't leave hair all over your furniture, and they don't give your home an unpleasant scent. A month's supply of batteries is much cheaper than a month's supply of dog or cat food.

INTERNET COMMENTS...

Here's a sampling of the kind of posts that were hitting the Internet in the days after Furby landed on planet earth...

"Does anyone know where I can get a Furby by trading? I have lots of beanie babies so I'd be glad to trade 3 or 4 of them for 1 Furby. I might actually even give the person $10 AND the 3 or 4 beanies!. PLEASE help me find a Furby!!" – Pat

"Hi, I have 4 Furby's and can't decide whether to give them to friends and relatives for Christmas or keep them for myself. I love my Furbys." – Susan

"I want to find a Furby so bad. Would someone please post where they found theirs? What is the most I should pay for one? The least?" – Stacey

"I want a Furby really bad and so do my friends. Please Santa get me one." – Karen

"I love Furby's. They are the best toy that has ever been made. I think Tickle Me Elmo is so stupid compared to a Furby." – Joe

"How can I stop my Furby Tah Dah from wanting to play hide and seek? He's wearing me out." – Bernadette

"Hey, I'm from Australia and I was wondering when I can get them over here? Because they are going to be HUGE! I can't wait." – Amanda

"I am the only one my Furby has to talk to. Will she get mad?" – Stan

"Furbys are awesome! I have 6. Their names are hard to remember so I made new names: Tidbit, Coal, Snow, Cuddles, Slushy, and Loudmouth." – Skippey

"Someone should start a service to help honest folks find a Furby at an honest price. And I don't mean collectors either. Let's get these things into the hands of the people they belong with, the children, not some money-grubbing baseball card dealer." – Willie

"I really want a Furby. I wrote many letters to Santa. I hope I get one." – Maggie

"I want a Furby SOOO bad, but dad just says, 'Sorry I don't think you are going to get one"...I want the riots to die down, but I bet when the crowd goes away there won't be any left. I really want one. Please help. I live in Missouri and I don't usually get caught in 'fads' like this, but I really do think the Furbys are a cool toy." – Furbydeprived

---

- A furby will definitely improve your attitude and put a smile on anyone's face. A Furby could break the tension in an argument or stressful meeting. If you're embarrassed to be playing with a toy, keep him a secret. He is small enough to hide in your glove compartment or desk, or pack in your bag for those long, boring trips. He'll always be there for you any time and place. Keep smiling!

FURBY
PARTY

THROW A PARTY!

- If you have friends with Furbys, invite them to a Furby Party. When you put 2 or more Furbys together, they'll play with each other. Start them talking by placing two or more Furbys in front of each other no more than 4 feet apart. Then tickle their tummies or pet their backs to get them talking. Give them a few minutes to get to know each other. If they don't start talking to each other, tickle their tummies again.

- They will talk, sing together (taking turns), and can even catch a cold from each other, which can be cured by feeding them 10-15 times. It will depend on how many Furbys you invite to the party, and what kind of mood each Furby is in. It is fun to see how many things they will do together. Sometimes they'll talk to each other so much you can't keep up with the conversation... this is especially true when there are four or more.

Put your Furbys in a circle and tickle them to get them started.
Sometimes it's hard to keep up with their conversations because they talk so fast!

FURBY PARTY

- They can even dance together. To start them dancing, place Furby on a hard surface like wood or tile, then clap your hands 4 times. If they don't start dancing right away, keep clapping. Once they get into dance mode you can keep them dancing simply by clapping again. When you stop clapping and they tire out, they'll say "me done". You can also use music to get them dancing — music with a strong dance beat works the best.

HIDE-N-SEEK

- Furbys love to play games. To play Hide N Seek, have everyone cover their eyes or leave the room while one person hides Furby. Like all kids, you must get Furby's attention so he knows you want to play. Pick him up and gently rock him from side to side a few times, then do the sequence to put him into Hide N Seek mode...

Cover his eyes briefly.... wait...

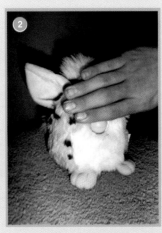

...cover his eyes briefly... wait...

...and repeat a total of four times.

- To play Hide-N-Seek, do the following actions:
    1. Cover his eyes briefly.
    2. Wait until he stops moving.
    3. Cover his eyes briefly.
    4. Wait until he stops moving.
    5. Cover his eyes briefly.
    6. Wait until he stops moving.
    7. Cover his eyes briefly.
    8. He'll say his name and "hide me" if done correctly.

- He'll remain quiet for 1 minute while you hide him. You (or your friend) will then have 3 minutes to find him. He will make a noise about every 10-15 seconds to help you find him. If you don't find him before time is up, he'll say "nah nah nah nah nah nah" several times. When you do find him and pick him up he'll do a little dance to show how happy he is.

- To stop playing Hide-N-Seek, turn him upside-down. Furby will say "Me done" to let you know the game is over.

OTHER GAMES FURBYS PLAY

- You can also have lots of fun playing Furby Says with your friends to see who can last the longest (see page 25) and Ask Furby (see page 23). You'll probably be able to think up other ways to play Furby with your friends.

Furby Trainer's Guide

FURBY PARTY

FURBY
BABY
REGISTRY

- Here's a place to keep all the information about your Furby. We've provided a few extra pages in case your lucky enough to have several Furbys. You can include all your Furbys "vitals", including name, date of birth, eye color, hair colors, and much more. You might want to make copies of the registry pages in case you need them for future Furbys.
- *Average Furby height is 5 1/2 inches, and weight is 11 oz.*

Furby Registry

NAME: _____ DATE OF BIRTH: _____

CITY AND STATE OF BIRTH: _____

NAME OF PARENT(S): _____

BIRTH WEIGHT: _____ BIRTH HEIGHT: _____

HOME ADDRESS: _____

EYE COLOR: _____ FUR COLOR: _____

BELLY COLOR: _____ FEET COLOR: _____

HAIR COLOR (ON TOP OF HEAD): _____

☐ TAIL   ☐ MANE   ☐ SPOTTED   ☐ STRIPED

FIRST FURBISH WORDS: _____

FIRST ENGLISH WORDS: _____

NOTES: _____

_____

_____

_____

_____

[ATTACH TAG HERE]

Furby Registry

NAME: _____ **DATE OF BIRTH:** _____

CITY AND STATE OF BIRTH: _____

NAME OF PARENT(S): _____

BIRTH WEIGHT: _____ **BIRTH HEIGHT:** _____

HOME ADDRESS: _____

EYE COLOR: _____ **FUR COLOR:** _____

BELLY COLOR: _____ **FEET COLOR:** _____

HAIR COLOR (ON TOP OF HEAD): _____

☐ **TAIL** ☐ **MANE** ☐ **SPOTTED** ☐ **STRIPED**

FIRST FURBISH WORDS: _____

FIRST ENGLISH WORDS: _____

NOTES: _____

_____

_____

_____

_____

[ATTACH TAG HERE]

Furby Registry

NAME: _____ DATE OF BIRTH: _____

CITY AND STATE OF BIRTH: _____

NAME OF PARENT(S): _____

BIRTH WEIGHT: _____ BIRTH HEIGHT: _____

HOME ADDRESS: _____

EYE COLOR: _____ FUR COLOR: _____

BELLY COLOR: _____ FEET COLOR: _____

HAIR COLOR (ON TOP OF HEAD): _____

☐ TAIL   ☐ MANE   ☐ SPOTTED   ☐ STRIPED

FIRST FURBISH WORDS: _____

FIRST ENGLISH WORDS: _____

NOTES: _____

_____

_____

_____

_____

[ATTACH TAG HERE]

The following pages include Adoption Certificates for your Furbys, suitable for framing!

You should never feed your baby real food — stick to the imaginary kind and they'll stay healthy. Spaghetti, for example, is a really bad idea!

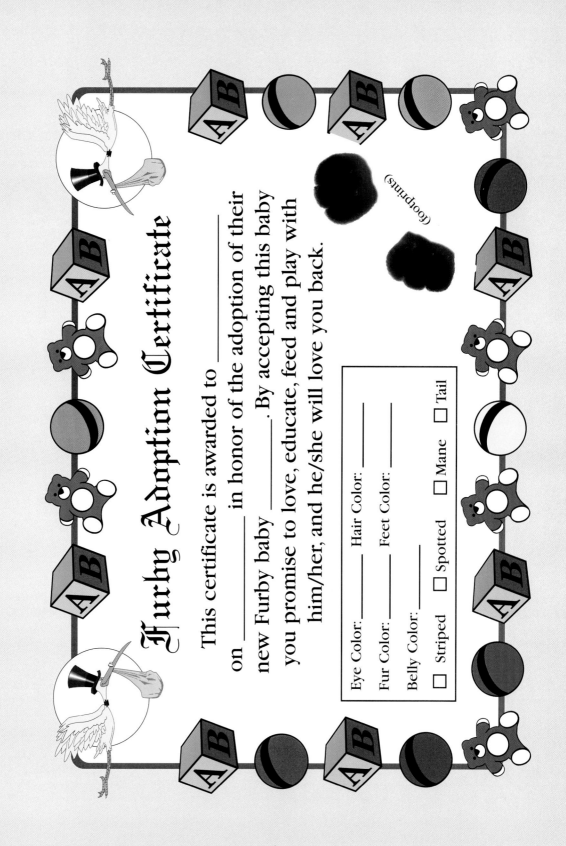

Furby Adoption Certificate

This certificate is awarded to _____

on _____ in honor of the adoption of their

new Furby baby _____. By accepting this baby

you promise to love, educate, feed and play with

him/her, and he/she will love you back.

(footprints)

Eye Color: _____   Hair Color: _____

Fur Color: _____   Feet Color: _____

Belly Color: _____

☐ Striped ☐ Spotted ☐ Mane ☐ Tail

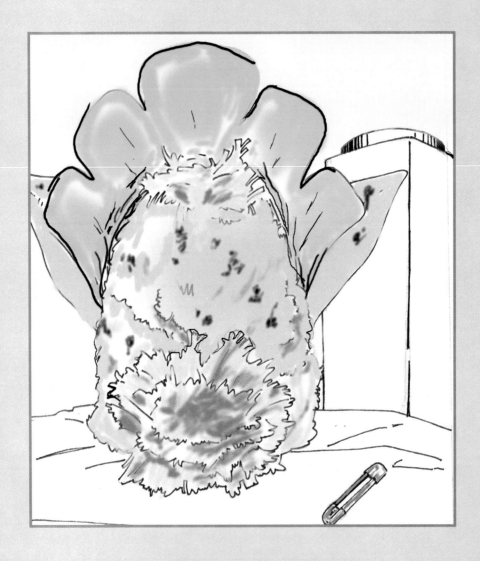

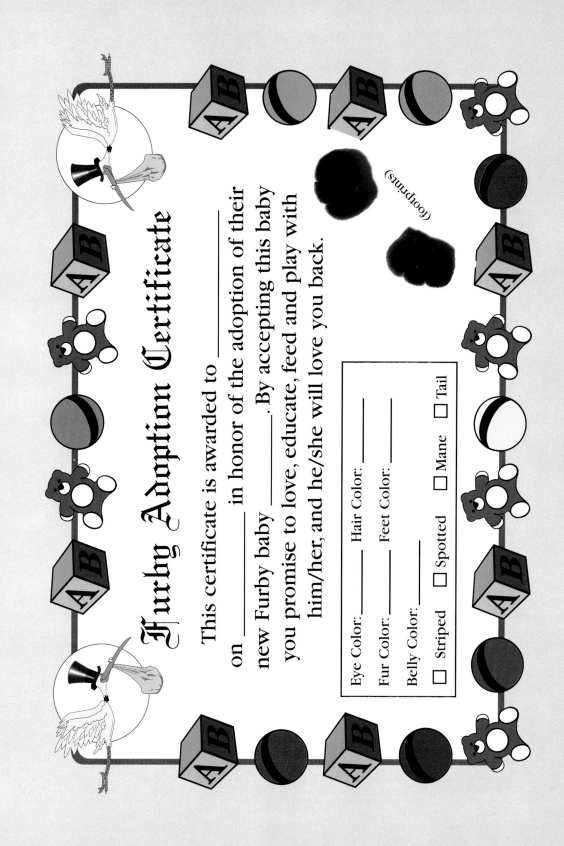

Furby Adoption Certificate

This certificate is awarded to _____

on _____ in honor of the adoption of their

new Furby baby _____. By accepting this baby

you promise to love, educate, feed and play with

him/her, and he/she will love you back.

(footprints)

Eye Color: _____   Hair Color: _____

Fur Color: _____   Feet Color: _____

Belly Color: _____

☐ Striped   ☐ Spotted   ☐ Mane   ☐ Tail

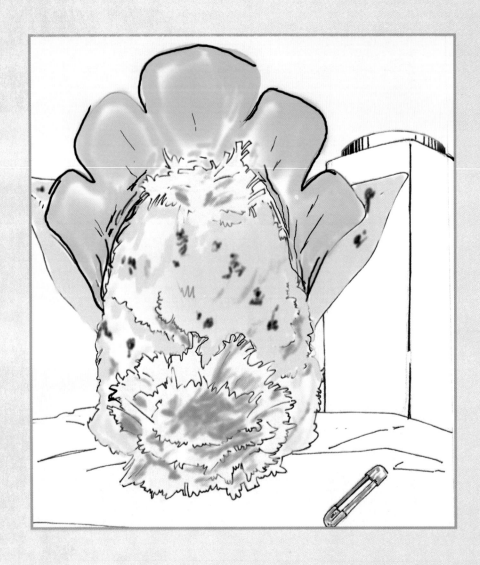

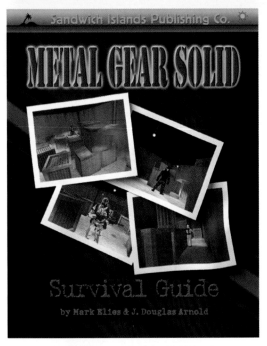
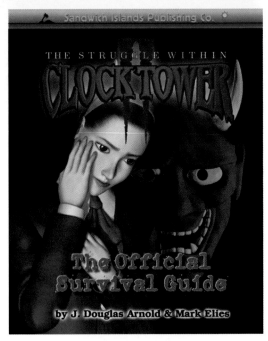

GAMEBOY SURVIVAL GUIDE:
1999 EDITION

by Cameron Davis
144 Pages • Available Now • $9.95
ISBN 1-884364-38-1

Over 350 titles are covered in this encyclopedic guide with reviews, codes and secrets for all your favorite GameBoy games. Includes a full walkthrough for Final Fantasy Legends 1, 2 and 3, plus Zelda.

POKéMON TRAINER'S
SURVIVAL GUIDE

by Mark MacDonald
144 Pages • Available Now • $9.95
ISBN 1-884364-29-2

In-depth and detailed information on every aspect of eachPokémon game product (including those not yet released in the US) and on all 151 monsters with complete walkthroughs for the RPG quests.

PLAYSTATION SURVIVAL GUIDE
VOLUME THREE

by J. Douglas Arnold and his team of experts
200 Pages • Available Now • $9.95
ISBN 9-781884-364402

Complete walkthroughs, strategies and tips for 11 of the hottest PlayStation games. Each chapter includes dozens of screen shots and step-by-step guides for beating the game. It's like getting 11 books in 1!

ORDER FORM

VIDEO GAME HINT AND SECRETS BOOKS

SEND TO:

Name _____

Address _____

City _____ State _____ Zip _____

Phone (_____) _____

Method of Payment:

( ) Check/Money Order ( ) MasterCard/Visa/Amex

Credit card users complete card information:

Card # _____ Expires: _____

Cardholder's Signature: _____

TITLE	ISBN	PRICE	x QTY	= TOTAL
Furby Trainer's Guide	(1-884364-42-X)	$11.95	_____	$ _____
Best of Maui (hardbound guide)	n/a	$12.00	_____	$ _____
Clock Tower: The Struggle Within Official Guide	(1-884364-28-4)	$12.95	_____	$ _____
Armored Core: Project Phantasma Official Guide	(1-884364-32-2)	$12.95	_____	$ _____
Metal Gear Solid Survival Guide	(1-884364-31-4)	$12.95	_____	$ _____
Castlevania Survival Guide (PlayStation)	(1-884364-36-5)	$12.95	_____	$ _____
Final Fantasy VII Survival Guide	(1-884364-48-9)	$14.95	_____	$ _____
PlayStation Survival Guide: Volume 3	(1-884364-40-3)	$14.95	_____	$ _____
Pokémon Trainer's Survival Guide	(1-884364-29-2)	$9.95	_____	$ _____
GameBoy Survival Guide: 1999 Edition	(1-884364-38-1)	$9.95	_____	$ _____
Nintendo 64 Survival Guide: Volume 2	(1-884364-34-9)	$14.95	_____	$ _____
Yoshi's Story Survival Guide	(1-884364-43-8)	$12.95	_____	$ _____
StarFox 64 Survival Guide	(1-884364-41-1)	$12.95	_____	$ _____
Nintendo 64 Survival Guide (Vol. 1)	(1-884364-45-4)	$14.95	_____	$ _____
Super Mario 64 Survival Guide	(1-884364-19-5)	$12.95	_____	$ _____
Tekken 1 & 2 Survival Guide	(1-884364-47-0)	$12.95	_____	$ _____
3DO Games Secrets, Books 1 & 2	Special Offer!	$19.95	_____	$ _____
Atari Jaguar Official Games Secrets	(1-884364-13-6)	$16.95	_____	$ _____
Mortal Kombat 3 Player's Guide	(1-884364-14-4)	$12.95	_____	$ _____
Yoshi's Island Strategy Guide	(1-884364-21-7)	$12.95	_____	$ _____
Awesome Sega Genesis Secrets 3, 4 & 5	Special Offer!	$19.95	_____	$ _____

Sub-Total: $ _____

Air Shipping ($4.00 U.S. and Canada TOTAL; $5.00 Foreign PER BOOK in U.S. FUNDS): $ _____

Total: $ _____

MAIL, FAX OR SEND TO:
SANDWICH ISLANDS PUBLISHING
P.O. Box 10669, Lahaina, HI 96761
Fax: (808) 661-2715
Phone Orders: (808) 661-8195

See our web site for updated information,
detailed listings, and special offers!

www.gamebooks.com